Binks the elf was preparing to visit
her cousins for a week.

"The forest will get very messy while
I'm away," said Binks. "I had better make
a list of jobs for everyone to do."

So she wrote out a long list of jobs.

2

3

Dash's job was to keep the forest
paths clean. She had to use her long tail
like a brush.

"Yuk!" groaned Dash. "The dirt is getting
stuck in my tail!" But she had promised
to help, so she finished
the job.

4

5

READ

Read pages 6 to 7

Purpose: To find out what Tufty's job is and what she thinks of it.

EXPLORE

Pause at page 7

Why do you think Tufty says it seems silly to trim the trees with her beak?

Do you think she is right?

 Use these questions to gain evidence for AF3.

Why does she help anyway? Is her reason the same as Dash's?

Check that the children can read the medium frequency words 'wanted', 'know', 'why' and 'would'.

 Use this pointer to gain evidence for AF1.

READ

Read pages 8 to 11

Purpose: To find out what Boo and Hector think of their jobs.

Tricky words (pages 8 and 10)

If the children struggle with 'favourite' (page 8), 'supposed' (page 8) or 'ridiculous' (page 10), encourage them to split these words into syllables and blend all through each syllable to read the words. Help them with the tricky parts of each word, e.g. the long 'a' in 'favourite', the long 'o' in 'supposed' and the end of 'ridiculous'. (AF1)

Tufty had a job to do too. "I don't know why Binks wanted me to trim all these trees with my beak," she said.
"It seems a bit silly to me. But I did say I would help, so I'd better get on with it, I suppose."

6

7

Binks left a job for Boo as well.
He had to tidy his favourite cave.
It was a long, hard job.

"I liked my cave the way it was," he moaned. "Monsters' caves are supposed to be dark and gloomy."

8

9

5

EXPLORE

Pause at page 11

What job does Boo have to do?

Why doesn't Boo really like this job?

How does Hector feel about his job?

Do you think Binks was right to ask Hector to mend his bridge?

READ

Read pages 12 and 13

Purpose: To find out what job Nuggle has to do.

EXPLORE

Pause at page 13

Why doesn't Nuggle want to get rid of her old webs?

How do you think all Binks' friends are feeling about her at this point?

 Use this question to gain evidence for AF3.

Please turn to page 14 for Revisit and Respond activities.

READ

Lesson 1

Read pages 2 to 5

Purpose: To find out how Binks tries to make sure all the jobs get done while she is away.

EXPLORE

Pause at page 5

What does Binks do to make sure the others do the jobs while she is away?

What do you think the others will think of this?

What is Dash's job?

Do you think she is pleased to do it?

What is the problem with Dash's job?

Why does Dash do her job anyway?

Tricky words (page 2)

If the children struggle with 'preparing', encourage them to split this word into syllables to read it. Check that they know what the word means. Help the children if necessary with the tricky 'ou' grapheme in 'cousins'. (AF1)

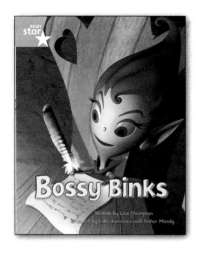

Front cover

Read the title together: 'Bossy Binks'.

What kinds of things do you think Binks might do in this story?

Why do you think the title says she is 'bossy'?

Back cover

Let's read the blurb together.

Who do you think will help Binks keep the forest tidy?

Do you think the others will be keen to help, or do you think they might prefer not to?

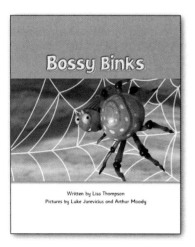

Title page

Does this page give us any clues about what will happen in this story?

Can you find the names of the author and illustrators?

1

"This is ridiculous!" muttered Hector.
"Binks says my bridge is dangerous, just
because some of the stones are falling off.
I think it's fine just the way it is."

Hector grumbled and groaned, but he fixed
the bridge anyway.

10

11

Nuggle's job was to tidy up some of her
old webs.

"Oh dear!" she sighed. "I'm very fond of
all my webs, even the old ones. I don't
really want to lose any of them."

But she had promised to help, so
she found some tatty old webs to
pull down.

12

13

LESSON 2

Recap lesson 1

What does Binks do to make sure all the jobs are done when she goes away?

What do Binks' friends think about this plan?

Can you remember some of the jobs they do?

Why do they agree to do the jobs even though they are not keen?

 Use this question to gain evidence for AF3.

READ

Read pages 14 to 17

Purpose: To find out how the characters begin to change their minds about the list of jobs.

EXPLORE

Pause at page 17

What job did Gog have to do?

How did he change his mind about it?

How do you think the other characters felt when they realised it was easier to walk in the forest now?

 Use these questions to gain evidence for AF3.

There was a big job for Gog on the list.
He had to weed his vegetable garden.

"This garden looks all right to me,"
said Gog. "I don't think it needs
weeding. But Binks is my friend,
so I'll do it to please her."

Gog began weeding in the morning and
kept at it all day. Then he looked around.
"Hey, perhaps Binks was right!" he said.
"It does look better without any weeds!"

In the forest, everyone noticed the difference.
Now that the paths were clear and the trees
were trimmed, it was much easier to walk.
No one tripped over or got scratched by
branches.

Read pages 18 to 21

Purpose: To find out what good things happen as a result of doing the jobs on the list.

Pause at page 21

What is the good thing about getting rid of Nuggle's webs?

What can she do now?

How is Gog's vegetable garden improved?

What do you think Binks will think when she comes back?

Check that the children can read high and medium frequency words such as 'going' and 'ever' fluently on sight.

 Use this pointer to gain evidence for AF1.

Now that Nuggle's old webs were gone, there was lots of space between the trees.

"I'm going to make my biggest and best ever web now!" said Nuggle.

In Gog's garden, all the vegetables were growing bigger and better than ever.

"The vegetables have much more room to grow, now that the weeds are gone," said Gog.

READ

Read pages 22 and 23

Purpose: To find out what happens at the end of the story.

EXPLORE

Pause at page 23

What happens when Binks comes back?

Why don't the others notice her?

How do you think Binks feels?

Is she upset or pleased that the others have been doing their jobs?

 Use these questions to gain evidence for AF3.

READ

Read page 24

Purpose: To answer the questions.

EXPLORE

Pause at the end

Share and discuss the children's answers to the questions on page 24.

The forest looked so good that everyone decided to keep on doing their jobs every day. They were so busy sweeping, cleaning and fixing things that they didn't even notice when Binks came back.

"Here I am!" she called. "Did you miss me?"

"We haven't had time to miss you," grumbled Hector. "We've been too busy!"

"I should go on holiday more often," remarked Binks with a smile.

22

23

Think About!

Do you do any jobs to help out at home?

How did everyone feel about having to do their jobs?

What changed their minds about the jobs in the end?

24

13

After Reading

Revisit and Respond

Lesson 1

- Check that the children are able to read most of the words in the text fluently on sight, by asking them to read pages 2 to 13 aloud as a group, with one child reading the pages about each character (Binks, Dash, Tufty, Boo, Hector, Nuggle). Encourage them to pay attention to the punctuation and read with pace and fluency. (AF1)

- Talk about how Binks feels when she sets out on her trip. Why does she think she has to leave a list for the others? How do the others feel about their jobs? Do the children think Binks is being bossy, or is she being sensible? How would they feel, if they were one of the forest creatures? (AF3)

- Write Binks' name at the centre of a spider diagram or mind map. As a group, try to think of some good words to describe her, as well as 'bossy'. Remind the children to think about the way she looks, the things she does and the things she says. You could use some of the words to write a brief character description of Binks. (AF3)

Lesson 2

- Make a list of some of the high and medium frequency words from the book that you would like the children to focus on, e.g. 'everyone', 'use', 'would' and 'because'. Read out the words one at a time without showing them to the children, and challenge them to find the words in the book. Then ask the children to close their books and see if they can spell the words as you read them out. (AF1)

- On the board or flipchart, draw two columns and write 'at the start of the story' at the top of one column and 'at the end of the story' at the top of the other. Talk about how some of the characters felt at the start and end of the story (e.g. Binks, Hector, Gog, Nuggle) and write brief notes about their feelings in each column. Ask the children why they think the characters' feelings have changed. (AF3)

- Ask the children what they think will happen next at the end of the story. Do they think the others will carry on doing their jobs, even now Binks is back? Or will they go back to the way they were? (AF3)

Follow-up

Independent Group Activity Work

This book is accompanied by two photocopy masters, one with a reading focus and one with a writing focus, which support the main teaching objectives of the book. The photocopy masters can be found in the *Fantastic Forest Planning and Assessment Guide.*

PCM Gold F 1.1 (*reading*)
PCM Gold F 1.2 (*writing*)

You may also like to invite the children to read the story again, during their independent reading (either at school or at home).

Writing

Guided writing Write a postcard from Binks to her forest friends while she is away. You could include a description of her holiday and some questions about whether the forest is being kept tidy.

Extended writing Write a follow-up to the story. Will Binks' friends carry on doing their jobs? Will they think of some extra jobs they can do as a surprise for her? Or will they give up doing their jobs and let the forest get messy again?

Assessment Points

The questions in this Teaching Version will help you to assess children's attainment within a range of Assessment Focuses (AFs), but particularly AF1 and AF3. See the *Fantastic Forest Planning and Assessment Guide* for more information about the AFs.

Word Recognition and Language Comprehension

- Check that the children can read medium frequency words such as 'wanted', 'everyone' and 'because' fluently on sight. (AF1).

- Check that the children can tell you how the feelings of the main characters change during the story and why. (AF3)